# Block chain

## *A Beginners Guide to Mastering the Hidden Economy*

*Block Chain*

# Table of Contents

| | |
|---|---|
| Chapter One: Block chain | 1 |
| Chapter Two: The History of Block chain | 4 |
| Chapter Three: How to use Block chain | 6 |
| Chapter Four: How to Invest using Block Chain | 9 |
| Chapter Five: Pros and Cons of Block Chain | 12 |
| Chapter Six: Bitcoin on Block chain | 15 |
| Chapter Seven: Cryptocurrency | 17 |
| Chapter Eight: Smart Contracts | 20 |
| Chapter Nine: Cryptographic Methods | 30 |
| Chapter Ten: Disruption of the Financial Service Industry | 32 |
| Chapter Eleven: Misconceptions of Block chain | 34 |
| Chapter Twelve: Myths about Block Chain and Bitcoin | 40 |
| Chapter Thirteen: Block chain terms | 44 |
| Chapter Fourteen: Block chain and Etherum | 48 |
| Conclusion | 51 |

# Introduction

I would like to thank you as well as congratulate you for downloading the book *Block chain*.

This book is going to give you the steps that you will need in order to master the world of block chain and make it work for you. Not only that, but you are going to learn all that you need to know about block chain.

An inescapable factis that you are going to know everything there is to know about block chain and will know if investing in block chain is something that you are going to want to get into.

In developing your skills on block chain, you are going to learn about a secret economy that not many are a part of. You will learn the ins and outs of block chain and how block chain will be beneficial to you in the long run.

It is now time for you to become an expert on the hidden economy of block chain!

# Chapter One: Block chain

Block chain is a database that holds a list of records. This database cannot be tampered with or revised and is constantly growing.

This database contains data structured in blocks that hold data as well as programs that are more recent implementations. Each individual block holds its own copy of transactions that have been done along with the results of any actions that were executed with it.

Each block in a block chain is a record of any time stamped and valid transaction that was made. In order to link the blocks together, the next block in line contains a hash from the previous block. This, in turn, links the blocks with a chain. This is how the database got its name block chain.

The blocks enter and log the sequenced transactions into the block chain. These blocks are created by the users aka miners that are using specialized equipment or software that is designed to create blocks.

Block chain is based all on transactions which the business dictionary describes as an "agreement or transfer of cash or property that occurs between two or more parties and establishes a legal obligation."

Block chain is the big technical innovation when it comes to bitcoin. Block chain acts as the public ledger in any and all transactions done with bitcoin. When a new user connects to a new network or creates a new transaction, a new block is made. This process is called permissionless.

Block chain works off of two different records which are transactions along with the blocks.

## Block Chain

Transactions consist of information that is actually stored in the block chain. Any and all transactions are created because of the participants that are using the system. Anytime that an owner of cryptocurrency sends some currency to another user, a transaction has been created.

These transactions pass node to node. Any system that is implementing the block chain actually defines a confirmed transaction is. In order for a transaction to be verified, it must be signed and spend at least one unspent output based on previous transactions as well as include the total of any transaction output. But, the outputs cannot exceed the sum of the inputs.

Miners are giving incentives in a cryptocurrency system so they are able to continue the creation of blocks. Miners can collect two kinds of rewards, either a pre-defined per-block award or a fee that is payable to any miner who can successfully confirm the transaction.

Block chain allows innovation and testing of virtual currencies such as altcoins (which are the competitors for bitcoin), as well as any other crypto-currencies while trying to improve one of all its aspects. Sites like Litecoin have a higher coin limit that is allowed as well as more blocks generated which results in more transactions being verified at a quicker rate.

In London, a candidate for mayor wanted to register the city budget with block chain so that public fundings would be accessed by the general public so that they could see where the money was going. A report by the World Economic Forum said that by 2025 73.1% could expect the first government tax to be collected by block chain. Also, about 10% of the global gross domestic products would be able to be stored on block chain.

## *Block Chain*

Block chain's original inspiration was for such things as cryptocurrencies (which we will discuss later) and other distributed databases. Much like the internet, block chain is being developed and transformed to be more user-friendly.

# Chapter Two: The History of Block chain

In 2008 Satoshi Nakamoto was the original publisher as well as the original source code for bitcoin later in 2009. Nakamoto's design became the inspiration for such things as cryptocurrencies as well as other distributed databases. When April of 2014 more than 80 cryptoledgers used Nakamoto's block chain design.

As well as the eighty cryptoledgers, block chain 2.0 was the newest term in the block chain database field. Along with this, came eight funded projects that were to use block chain 2.0 were started.

Implementing the second generation of block chain was described as a language that allowed users to write sophisticated contracts which in turn creates invoices that are paid when a shipment arrived or even when shared certificates automatically sent their owners the dividends when profits reached a certain point.

Basically block chain is a database that works within itself to help make the use of programs easier for their users by doing things that the user would normally do, thus making it easier for the userto have access to the database without having to worry aboutthings not being set up and sent out on time.

As of 2016, a new project using block chain technology was announced to be launched for the central securities of the Russian Federation. Other regulated bodies such as the music industry have also tested models using block chain in order to collect things such as royalties as well as manage their copyrights worldwide.

## *Block Chain*

In order to support new assets and utilize the transactional currency, bitcoin-based subchains became possibly by linking chains. This also means that even though there are multiple chains in one block, new bitcoins were not created.

# Chapter Three: How to use Block chain

There are two differentways that you can use block chain. You can use block chain as an individual or as a merchant. This section willshow you how you can use block chain as an individual. It will take you step by step of what is needed for you to use it properly.

**Using block chain as an Individual:**

**One:** Setting up your wallet.

Normally you would keep your money in your wallet for safe keeping. However, you cannot put digital money in your wallet. That is why you need a digital wallet. This wallet is a private account where your bitcoins will be stored.

Mobile Wallets: these bitcoin wallets are going to run on any mobile device. These wallets are great for in store use. Being that mobile devices are harder to hack, than a computer is, it will create a secure environment for you to store your bitcoins. Two good mobile wallets are Mycelium and Airbitz.

Software wallets: these do not depend on any third party service after it has been downloaded. The wallet will operate on your computer, but you will need to run your transactions anonymously. Bitcoin was originally created for this wallet type. Some of the recommended software wallets are Multibit and Armory.

Web wallets: web wallets are more user-friendly as well as convenient being that you will always have access to them when you have access to the internet. It is as simple as creating an account and then logging in. these are less secure than a hardware wallet. Some good web wallets are Coinjar, EasyWallet, Block chain, and Coinbase.

**Two:** acquire bitcoins.

The process of getting bitcoins is not simple, but there are a variety of options that you are able to use to get bitcoins. Since the system is unpredictable and experimental, there are several unique opportunities. In order to gather bitcoins, you can:

Trade bitcoins: by looking for other participants of bitcoin, you can find someone that is interested in a transaction. These participants are going to be found on trading sites. You will also be able to sell goods or even services and get bitcoins.

Purchase bitcoins: visiting a bitcoin marketplace you are able to make purchase bitcoins. Simple transactions will allow you to spend money in order to have it converted into bitcoins.

Mine bitcoins: mining programs are available to be downloaded so you are able to use a custom CPU in orderto make a quick profit by simply sitting at your computer. This technique was used when bitcoin was first starting out, but, is not easy to get to now.

**Three:** Secure your wallet.

Having coins is going to put you at risk for someone trying to steal them. It is advised that you secure your wallet so you are protecting yourself and the coins that you have earned or purchased. Older clients of bitcoin did not encrypt their wallet data, so everyone had access to steal each other's coins. Now, you can run encryption programs in order to protect your coins. You can also keep different wallets so that there is one that you use for your daily transactions; and one to use as a savings account.

## *Block Chain*

**Four:** find different merchants who accept bitcoin.

Bitcoin can be used as any normal currency is. You have acess to have a credit or debit card that has access to the bitcoin wallet that is in your name. However, you need to find the right merchants that actually accept bitcoins.

## Chapter Four: How to Invest using Block Chain

Block chain is a hot trend as of right now. It has the potential to be able to transform business models in a high number of businesses. You will find that block chain is similar to a digital spreadsheet that all members on a decentralized network have access to.

Investors that are looking at how they can tap into the profit that is just sitting underneath the surface with block chain technology. With how block chain is written out, you will need to think about the unique factors that you are going to find when it comes to block chain; it is nothing like traditional trading. There are several levels that will allow you to leverage the potential that is behind block chain.

With this being said, there are at least five ways that you are able to invest using block chain.

**One**: Stockpile bitcoins:

Many investors have taken advantage of stockpiling gold in hoping the price will rise in the near future. However, other investors have taken to stockpiling bitcoins. While the two assets are extremely different, the same basic investing techniques and principals are going to apply.

For example, both assets are going to be considered rare. The rate that bitcoin was generated in the beginning days of the program was actually fast, and as the years have passed, the rate has decreased while the technology has reached the built in limit of twenty-one million coins.

In the end, it is going to come down to supply and demand. If the supply is limited but the demand is increasing, then the value of the asset is going to increase.

**Two:** Block chain penny stocks

Penny stocks are quite common, and there are even penny stocks in cryptocurrency. Bitcoin is actually a well known digital currency. However this is not the only option. Along with Ether coins, there are coins such as Litecoin and Altcoins. As time as gone on, other digital currencies were developed to compete with bitcoin. While this is going on, some currencies are used to fill the needs that bitcoin does not meet.

For example, there are cryptocurrencies that are being and have been developed to help enable a digital asset registry by providing an increase in security for the asset through allowing escrow services as well as other ways that privacy can be enhanced.

The bitcoin penny stocks are going to offer investment opportunities.

**Three:** Altcoin crowdfunding

Crowdfunding is considered to be a mainstream method that is used for raising seed capital when it comes to various investments. So, instead of using coins, you can use crowdfunding when you choose to get involved with bitcoin. To use this method, you will need to have coins that are supplied through pre-mining and then they will be sold during an initial coin offering; this is done before the system was launched publicly.

Bitshares are also a well-known method to be used when getting started using block chain. The apps and services are going to be utilized in a pre-sale method as an effort to raise the funds that are needed. Investors are ultimately given the chance to purchase coins knowing that at some point in time, the price will increase should the service become more popular.

**Four:** Angel funding and start-up ventures

Angel funding, as well as start-up ventures, are not a new concept. However, a variation that has begun to take hold is that there is the idea that you can invest in startups that are already built using block chain technology. While block chain has become increasingly popular, there are a number of entrepreneurs that have begun to show interest in experimenting with the technology that is behind cryptocurrency.

Just like any new venture, all startups are going to need some sort of funding. If you are given the funding by using angel funding, then you could very well end up having the next block chain frontier.

It should be understood that you will face risks risks no matter what you attempt to start up. But, since the profits are going to have the potential to be substantial, it is wise to carefully think about the pros and consof what you are trying to start up.

**Five:** Pure block chain technology play

There are a number of block chain technologies that are now on the rise. Companies such as BTCS, Inc are becoming well-known names now thanks to block chain. For example, "pure play" with BTCS are going to focus on the block chain technology and work to secure the block chain through distinctive transactions that are verified through the verification services.

Global Arena Holding is the company that is currently leveraging block chain technology in order to get voting verification.

# Chapter Five: Pros and Cons of Block Chain

There are a variety of different things that you can do with block chain. But, why in the world are you going to want to choose block chain if you are not aware of the pros and cons of it? We have talked about what block chain is, how it works, and many other things that are useful to know when it comes to understanding block chain.

As a consumer, bitcoin is going to not only protect your identity but your money as well. You will not have to disclose any of your personal information when you are completing a bitcoin transaction; it is a lot like cash.However, you will not need to give a credit card number that has the possibility of being stolen. To help with your anonymity, you will use your bitcoin address. This address changes with every transaction that you make.

You are also able to receive and send payments at virtually no cost. When you make international payments, you will not need to pay a foreign transaction fee or exchange fee. This is very useful when you are traveling.

On the opposite hand, you are unable to reverse any transactions that you make. The only way to get the coins that you spend back is if the individual that received the funds refunds them to you. Therefore, if you accidentally send it to the wrong address, there is no recourse for it. You also cannot get any liability protection when it comes to bitcoin usage. In that case, you will have to deal with the loss should your wallet get stolen.

## Block Chain

Should you decide to hold on to your bitcoins, then you are going to be forced to deal with their volatility. Bitcoins can fluctuate a lot over the time period that you keep them. For example, the price of bitcoins can range from 1,200 to 600 dollars. There is a chance that you are going to be able to make a profit from the speculations, but you may also lose a considerable amount of money.

Companies like TigerDirect and Etsy had gotten on board when it comes to accepting bitcoins. However, companies like Target and Walmart have not gotten on board.

The bitcoins are going to be similar to cash instead of credit cards. As far as credit cards go, you are able to have warranty extensions, earn rewards points, have liability protection, and even have the comfort of knowing if your card is will be accepted or not. But, credit cards can because you are to acquire late fees, foreign fees, and it can also affect your credit score. But, with cash, it is accepted everywhere, and it will not factor into other parts of your life such as your credit score. Like with bitcoin, you are able to use it without having to worry about late fees and such. Sadly, it is not accepted at all retailers.

When it comes to being a business and using bitcoin, you are saving yourself money. If youuse a service such as Coinbase, the first million dollars that you earn free from any fees. But, from there, you will pay one percent on all transactions that are made. This is a major saving compared to the usual three to four percent that you can get from credit cards.

Most exchanges are going to convert bitcoin payments in order to minimize your risk of volatility. Along with that, using bitcoin is going to help in easing the worry of charge backs, PCI compliance, and hackers that tend to go after credit card numbers. Many bitcoin merchants use a tablet

## Block Chain

or smartphone in order to process the payments that they receive; this is a major plus because you are not going to need an expensive POS system as well as the hardware that comes with it.

With this, you need to establish a clear policy when it comes to refunding items and returns on items that have been bought with bitcoins. You need to base the return amount on the dollar price of the item instead of the bitcoin price that you sold the item for. This way you are not exposing yourself to bitcoin's volatility.

In the end, it is recommended that you keep up to date with the development of bitcoin so that you are not left in the dark about the new technology that comes out. Do not allow sensationalized headlines cloud your assessment of cryptocurrency and your decision on if you want to use it. When you accept a mixture of payments you are going to be able to lower the risk of identity theft and possible stolen card information along with getting more customers in the door while helping to save on any processing fees you may occur. Not only that, but, you will be defending yourself against hackers in a way that is similar to the way a consumer would be able to protect themselves.

# Chapter Six: Bitcoin on Block chain

Any and all public records for bitcoin transactions are kept on a block chain. This allows a novel solution without needing a trusted central authority; thus maintenance that is needed to the block chain is done by the network that is running bitcoin software. For example, a transaction in the form of x sends y bitcoins to the payee which is z, therefore, is broadcasted to the network when the software applications are available.

These networks validate the transactions to make sure they are valid before adding them to the ledger and giving additional nodes the broadcast of the transaction. In order to achieve the independent verification that bitcoin needs, block chain works as a distributed database. Therefore, each bitcoin and network node will store its own data in the block chain.

A block is created approximately six times an hour when the new transactions are accepted, verified, and then accepted into the chain. In doing this, the software will be allowed to determine when a certain amount of bitcoin has been spent which is going to help prevent double-spending. This is particularly helpful because this is an environment that has no central oversight of what happens.

A conventional ledger would record any transfers of promissory notes or actual bills that will exist apart from the network. Bitcoins coins can only exist in the form of an unspent output transaction in the block chain.

So, in conclusion, a miner creates a new block and as well as any maintenance that needs to be done is done, and the

## Block Chain

miner is given a reward for their work. Miners are also rewarded for the verification of transactions that are stored within the blocks.

# Chapter Seven: Cryptocurrency

Cryptocurrency is otherwise known as crypto currency or even crypto asset. This is a medium of exchange that is used to control the making of the new units through secure transactions. Cryptocurrency is an alternate currency which is actually a digital currency much like bitcoin. Ultimately, bitcoin was the first in order to decentralize the cryptocurrency back in 09. Since then, several cryptocurrencies have been created such as altcoins. Altcoins are actually a blend of bitcoins alternative.

As stated, cryptocurrency is decenteralized which means that it is much like the block chain used by bitcoins transaction database as far as using a distributed ledger goes. This also means that it does not run like normal banking systems that are centralized.

An anonymous electronic cash system was first published back in 1998 by Wei Dai which was called "b-money." Not too long after that, a Nick Szabo created what was known as "Bit Gold." Much like bitcoin, Bit Gold requires its users to complete work functions with solutions that are put together and published. A currency system that was based on the reusable proof of work. Was created by Hal Finney who used Wai and Szabo's work as inspiration.

Bitcoin that was created by Nakamoto used a cryptographic hash function (SHA-256) that allowed it to work as a proof of work system. Alternatively, in 2011 another system called Namecoin was created as an attempt to help DNS decentralize. In doing this, it would make the internet censorship extremely hard. Not too long after Namecoin was released, Litecoin was also released. This became the first cryptocurrency to use script as its hash function. Even again, a hybrid that used proof of work in addition to using proof of stake was created and ended up being called Peercoin.

Although several different cryptocurrency programs have been created, very few have actually ended up being successful. Back in August of 2014, the treasury department in the UK announced that they had been studying cryptocurrencies and what role they could end up playing in the UK economy.

Also in 2014 the second generation of cryptocurrency programs such as Monero, Ethereum, as well as NXT was presented to the public. These programs have some advanced functions that they use such as side chains, smart contracts, and stealth addresses.

On February 20,2014 the very first bitcoin ATM was launched by Jordan Kelley (who is the founder of Robocoin). This ATM is located in Austin, Texas and is just like a bank ATM, but the scanners instead read some form of government idea in order to confirm their identification. This ATM was used just like any other bank ATM, except that it would allow the user to gain access to any cryptocurrency that they had in their account.

Just like block chain, cryptocurrencies are threatening the price of credit for the financial institutes. Along with this, the more trade that happens with cryptocurrencies is going to inevitably cause the consumer to lose their confidence in fiat currencies. Because of the widespread use of cryptocurrencies, it is more difficult for financial institutions to gather data that they need as far as the economic activity is which is what helps the government to steer the economy.

It has been stated by a senior banking officer that the "widespread use of cryptocurrency makes it more difficult

*Block Chain*

for statistical agencies to gather the economical data that they require.

# Chapter Eight: Smart Contracts

Smart contracts are probably going to be the aspect of block chain that will most likely be championed in the future. A smart contract is a type of computer coding that is activated as soon as the block chain registers that a predetermined event has happened. The smart contract will have its own block and be added in as part of the chain.

While it may seem complicated, you can think of them in much the same way certain functions in a checking account work. In most checking accounts, automated deductions can be set up either by the user or by a third party with the user's permission. A smart contract works in broadly the same way, but from a decentralized—not centralized--position. Put another way; a smart contract is the computer code equivalent of the legalese in a contract that stipulates how and when all the little details are carried out.

Additionally, as long as the smart contract is generated on a public block chain, then, unlike in the banking example, there is no third party (such as the bank) who is able to step in and actively prevent the transaction from occurring. The transaction is equally secure if it is performed by a bank or by a block chain. This is due to the extreme type of security that is added into the block chain model, the fact that any data has been decentralized, and the extreme cost required to hijack a block chain.

What's more, unlike with traditional contracts, smart contracts that are executed via block chain are completely public and viewable by anyone with a copy of the chain. This means that the smart contract is never open for debate or discussion; it is purely an expression of the facts as they are truly stated. This can be seen as a blessing or a curse, of course, depending on the nature of the information being made public.

A smart contract is where a computer protocol can aid in the verification, and enforce the negotiation as well as the performance of a contract in which the contractual clause becomes unnecessary.

The smart contract contains a user interface that will mimic the logic of the contractual clause(s). The proponentsof a smart contract will claim a variety of differnt contractual clauses may be made partial or evenfully self-executing and self-enforcing, or possibly even both.

Smart contracts are going to aim to provide the security that is superior to any traditional law contract. This will, therefore, reduce the transaction costs that are associated with the process of drawing up a contract.

Even with all that being said, it is important to know a smart contract cannot retrieve data from the outside world. It can, however, ask outside sources to assist in the delivery of the information on its behalf. Even at that, it either can trust what the outside actor says or verify the information given. This is just like when in court, the judge will ask the experts about their opinion or if a witness testimony can be verified by cross-checking.

So, it is, therefore, obvious that the computational resources for block chain to "judge" can be restricted by gas limit, which is low rather when being compared to the powers of lawyers that work in the outside world. Even so, a judge can restrict a contract in such a way that a way can still be decided when it comes to very troubling legal case.

Ultimately, the contracts will be made on the system based on the data within the system. If any outside sources need to be consulted, the system will have to choose between verifying the information or just taking the source at its word. This is more beneficial because it takes a player a's wishes for what they want to be done and holds player b to it via the contract.

This is just like any other contract that is made in the outside world, but it is online. The system will be in place until player a gets the work from player b that they requested. This also works with the payment method because the payment will not be sent until the contractual agreements have been met.

**Common usage cases**

With the rising market penetration of various financial technologies, smart contracts are becoming more and more prevalent. A big reason for that is because they are simplifying many common contract usage cases. For example, they are already making it easier for users to update various contract terms in real time, despite it taking days for physical copies to move back and forth to perform the same function. This not only adds to the speed with which such processes can perform, but also increase the odds of their accuracy remaining at acceptable levels throughout.

Smart contracts also activate automatically once certain real world conditions have been met, which means they require fewer resources to be utilized to the fullest. While this won't mean much to most users who use them infrequently, for business to business transactions, the savings will likely be substantial. The guaranteed and secure nature of a smart contract also means that it can be executed upon without the need for a third party to guarantee the transaction via escrow, reducing the closing costs of the contract on all sides.

Financial institutions will also find smart contracts useful in numerous ways. In regard to trade clearing or settlement scenarios, the final results relating to settlements, transfers, and trades is tallied automatically. Smart contracts can be used when it comes to coupon payments, specifically to return principal on expired bonds. They also work with insurance claims as a means of minimizing errors and streamlining the flow of work between departments. Finally, they are also known to improve the regulation of Internet of Things services.

In the health care sector, smart contracts are known to offer up numerous advantages. For instance, they improve the accuracy with which medical records are updated as patients are transferred between departments. They can monitor the health of the population as a whole via public block chains that update automatically and pay participants for using their information. Smart contracts are also already in use in many Internet of Things devices where they are able to decide the success of fitness goals and release rewards accordingly.

In the music industry, smart contracts are already being put to work tracking royalties for song usage and distributing payments accordingly. It is also being put to work on a smaller scale to enhance person to person interactions and is predicted to lead to things like trading energy credits and increased peer lending opportunities.

## Block Chain

This same technology is currently being adapted for use with the Tesla electric car, whereby users can charge at any charging station and be billed for the transaction automatically.

It is also changing the way large products are shipped and tracked by sending out automated documentation as various production pieces make their way through processing, and on to shipping. This can even be cued to the input of certain signatures, meaning the process is seamless for signing the contract to receiving the goods. Later on down the line, if there are questions about the quality of the shipment, then the entire route the product took from creation to delivery can be tracked. This is because of the fact that it is on the same block chain that enables the creation of the contracts.

For credit enforcement, the smart contracts are becoming an extension of property law. The credit agreements are going to disable the product that you have purchased if you fail to make the payments that you agreed to make. For example, if you buy a new car on credit and fail to make your payment. Then the doors to your car are going to lock and then drive itself back to the show room. However, most electrical products come with what is known as a kill switch that can be disabled should a condition not be met between the two parties. This would happen if the payments were being made through a public channel such as cryptocurrency.

Being that s computer program cannot reliably tell you what is happening in the physical world, or who is telling the truth is the biggest limitation with smart contracts. So, in checking to see if a bitcoin payment was made is a simple task that a computer can do. However, in most real-world contracts it is much harder for a computer to do. A smart contract's execution is going to be as good as its input. But, this is going to be difficult to figure out if the inputs are sufficient enough to do the job in such a way that both parties are going to trust.

The biggest solution to this is going to be to have oracles. Oracles are online service providers whose entire job is to broadcast the data that can be used as inputs made by smart contract writers.

For example, if an oracle broadcasts the new entries on a government registry of the most recent deaths. The contract can pull out those who just had a living will or those who died because of natural causes.

When it comes to property law, the cryptocurrency related to a set of smart contracts. These smart contracts are going to be able to enforce property law. The cryptographic techniques are used in order to make sure that only the owner of the cryptocurrency is the one who can spend it. There are already several decentralized assets that exist. But, broaden out the range of assets so that there are different digital assets to be traded within a single block chain. When it comes to physical products such as electronic controls, then the same principle can be applied.

An early example of a smart contract is the Digital Rights Management otherwise known as DRM technologies. This contract does not take or even process the inputs. However, it does enforce itself by making it impossible for you to be able to break your contract by acting in an unauthorized manner. For example, copying something that is protected by copyright laws.

Finally, smart contracts also have the potential to make the voting process run more smoothly because smart contracts could verify a person's identity before recording their information. This information is safe from tampering, and can be easily recalled if a situation arises that calls for a closer examination.

**Financial sector**

A smart contract works on what is known as a single ledger system, which makes it extremely easy for the program in question to determine if a specific piece of information is accurate or if it should be completely ignored. When implemented properly, they allow for the automatic approval of workflow and verification of calculations which, as a result, reduces lag and the potential for error. At the same time, it minimizes the cost and completion time of projects of all types.

Smart contracts also help with clearing trades, as I briefly mentioned earlier. As you may know, clearing trades manually is a process that is typically quite intensive. It involves a lot of labor time, and can even necessitate quite a few reconciliations both internally and externally. What's worse, each reconciliation brings with it, its own chance for discrepancies, which result in extra delays that cost even more time and additional resources. However, smart contracts smooth out this process considerably, as all the changes will be noted and updated automatically. The number of these types of transactions that are performed each year number in the billions, which means the market is primed and ready for smart contract intervention.

The single ledger format also makes it easier for the multiple steps in any supply chain to move along smoothly. The way it does this is by easily allowing a product to go through all the logistical stops prior to delivery without extensive physical verification along the way. This will be a huge boon to supply chains of all shapes and sizes, being that physical document related mishaps are routinely responsible for delaying packages 20 percent of the time. Smart contracts will also be able to deal with letters of credit and bills of landing automatically, simply as the package makes its way towards its destination.

In addition to making errors at times, old-fashioned transaction monitoring systems cost more than 10 billion dollars each year, so adopting a smart contract system will save suppliers and merchants a significant amount in the long run. As such, numerous major players in nearly every industry are currently looking into what they can do in order for a smart contract system to be a reality in their field.

**Current limitations**

Block chain is the database infrastructure of the future, and smart contracts are going to be at the forefront of its expansion. It is essential that those who are wanting to use smart contracts to the fullest do what they can to prepare and promote new systems (their widespread use will end up being imminent). When looked at with a mindset towards the future, it is hard not to look at any process within a traditional business infrastructure that would not be improved by smart contracts that are deployed in the proper way.

Nevertheless, before you head out and begin investing exclusively in the smart contract market as it exists today, it is vital to understand that will be a few important issues that need to be resolved before the technology breaks through into the mainstream. First and foremost is the fact that many smart contract scenarios have been completed in usage scenarios that are small or medium-sized organizations; they are still largely untested in environments with a high volume of transactions such as in the traditional financial sector. If the public is ever going tofully accept the potential of smart contracts, they are going to need to see it working in action at the largest scale first.

Additionally, most smart contracts have no way of currently reaching information that is not stored within the block chain it is a part of. Some designers have discovered ways to include what are known as oracles, or access points to external information, into the smart contract, but the best way of doing so is still being discussed. This is not helped by the latency that a traditional distributed network faces, which can be as much as 20 seconds in some instances. While nowhere near the bottleneck it would have been a decade ago, this speed is still quite a bit longer than the milliseconds the same process could be completed in using a traditional server.

These issues combined have so far lead to few true examples of smart contracts being used in the real world. It's something else that needs to change if they are ever going to gain the wide acceptance they need to reach their true potential. What's more, the nature of how block chains store information means that once a contract has been written, it cannot be added to or amended in ways that were not in its base programming. The inability to make mistakes, especially while learning, will make it difficult for smart contracts to catch on without a mainstream reason for doing, so that appears viable in the long term.

Finally, one area where a traditional contract is still superior is privacy. While smart contracts created on private block chains don't have this issue, creating a smart contract on an open block chain means that everyone who is a part of that block chain will have the ability to see the details of the contract. This has potentially severe consequences for both individuals and businesses, as there is some information that the parties of a contract will naturally want to keep a secret. Until this matter is settled, the general use of smart contracts across many contract types is likely to remain low.

*Block Chain*

# Chapter Nine: Cryptographic Methods

Cryptographic methods are methods that are used in encrypting the data that is on the block chain. Two methods that can be used are hashing, timestamping and digital signatures. These methods are meant to provide you the assistance you need in order to encrypt the data that you want to keep from other block chain users.

**Hashing** is a public key encryption that uses the hash value. This value will compute the base impute by using the hashing algorithm. Basically, this will be a summary of the original value. Remember it is nearly impossible for you to be able to derive an original input if you do not know the data that was used in order to create the hash value.

For example your input number is 10,667

Your algorithm is going to be input# 143

Therefore, your hash value is going to be 1,525,381

It is difficult to understand how you got to that value, but you got to it by multiplying your input number by your input algorithm. If you only had 143, it would be simple for you to calculate and get the input number of 10,667.

However, public key encryption is more complex. Normally complex algorithms will be used for public key because large hash values are going to be used for encrypting. There can be 40 to 128-bit numbers. The 128-bit number is going to have a possibility of $2^{128}$ different combinations.

**Digital signatures** in block chain are going to provide ownership of funds. Basically, when an owner wants to send bitcoins to another user, then they be required to sign for the transaction, authorizing that they do indeed want to transfer the funds.

Then, this transaction is going to be sent to the public network on bitcoin and then recorded into the public database of block chain so that it can be verified through the digital signature.

Digital signatures each have a unique characteristic. One of these is a Multisig digital signature. This means there will be multiple private keys, and a quorum is going to be needed in order to use the funds. Traditional signatures are going to be contracted and signed by multiple people. However it cannot be enforced the m of n predefined signatures that are needed to complete the action.

This method is going to make it easier for audits to happen.

**Timestamping** is going to be different than the generally used digital signature. Transactions are going to be generated within ten minute periods which is an average block time. So, when a transaction is added to a block, it will be recorded and then it will be timestamped in order for the next participant to know when it was signed in order for it to be verified properly.

The time stamp is going to need to be trusted by a third party that is called Time Stamping Authorities. Their long term use actually helps with enternal maintenance in order to help preserve the validity of the timestamp.

# Chapter Ten: Disruption of the Financial Service Industry

Block chain startups are able to focus on start-up and the development of solutions that the financial industry is not able to. Block chain is also able to support crypto-currency as well as the financial services that their users need in order to use crypto-currency. Along with that, block chain allows financial assets to be tracked in a secure environment. Added to that it reduces the complexity and intermediaries that are involved when it comes to the transaction process. Block chain can also better help to manage the digital risks that are part of the financial industry. It will also create a ledger and help to distribute that to whom it needs to be distributed to as well as the processes that were used. Not to mention it can improve the process needed in order for the network to verify any historical transactions.

Since 2012, the start-up for bitcoin rose to around $1 billion and continues to rise. Because of this, some companies are attempting to break into the market while others are just trying to improve their current services. But, any bank is afraid to fully break through and become known as the blockbuster of the financial world.

With the new technology that is constantly evolving, it is possible that it can reduce the fees for any financial transaction as well as any risks that there are based on currency exchange. This can also help with payment faults or cut off times and will eliminate the need to duplicate any documentation.

Because of the growing technology, financial institutes are investing in block chain in order to set up internal teams as well as to invest in any startup companies.

## *Block Chain*

Block chain has the capability to reduce a lot of typical mistakes that are made in the financial industry. With the ability to handle payments, block chain can create a live document for the user and show them when the payment is due along with what is being paid out of their payment. Along with this, it will eliminate the need for the consumer and the bank to need documents. Block chain can hold the documents in a node that is easy to be accessed by the bank as well as the consumer. Not only that but when dealing with a startup company, block chain can use projections in order to show a financial service if it is worth investing in that specific company or not.

# Chapter Eleven: Misconceptions of Block chain

Many people do not fully understand how block chain works. There are misconceptions of block chain that people have not fully been able to understand because as we have mentioned, block chain is constantly changing to be more user-friendly and be able to help those who use it.

In this chapter, let's try and understand block chain a little more so that it is easier to understand.

**One: Block chains are secure**

Bitcoin actually has a specific set of security features that is used for writing data because of the proof of work consensus. Much like we stated earlier, in order for you to add blocks to block chain, you are going to need to validate all transactions within your block before you perform repeat calculations so that you can locate the number that makes your block acceptable to other block chain users as well as makes it valid. Along with the chain rule and proof of work, it is will be expensive on you to try mining your own subversive chain.

Private block chains are going to have other mechanisms that are going to replace the proof of work so that others are limited in their ability to subvert the chain that was created. This is can also be known as block validators.

But, the rules end up specifying which blocks are going to need to be signed by their known list of signatories. This list limited. The entries are going to take turns writing blocks so that there is enough done in a round robin fashion so that bad behavior is discouraged or at least limited.

## Two: Block chains are encrypted

Several different cryptographic methods are used with bitcoin as well as with the data that is encrypted and stored on block chain. Because of this, many people believe that all the data that is stored on block chain is encrypted, however, this is actually not true.

Most of the data that is on block chain is actually unencrypted being that the data will need to be validated by the nodes. So, you have the option to look at all the transaction data that is on the block chain servers.

But, the biggest problem with using encryption for any data is going to be that it cannot be validated by the nodes because the nodes are not going to be able to unencrypt the data and see what they should be validating.

While using a private chain, the nodes are going to be able to be decrypted through the use of decryption keys in decryption software. If you decide that you are going to do this, you are going to need to think about why you have decided to encrypt the data in the first place. What are the reasons that are pushing you towards thinking that you cannot place the data on the block chain server where all other users can have access to it?

Research with cryptographic is constantly revealing solutions that show that data that does not have any underlying data is known as zero knowledge proofs. When looking at this technology, you are going to come to realize that it is not fully matured yet.

Privacy is important to everyone, but what should you encrypt when it comes to blocking chain? Should the data that is in motion be encrypted? The data that is resting? Or should the whole database be encrypted? And then, when it is encrypted, who is going to have access to the data?

## Block Chain

When is it going to be decrypted? Can someone's permissions to the data be revoked?

Management of the data is crucial to the security of the data that is on the server. When the data is shared between two different parties, it is going to be even more crucial. So, carefully consider the security of the data that is in the block chain solution so that what needs to be protected is protected while still getting it validated by the nodes.

**Three: Block chain allows end users to erase the middle man and do peer to peer**

Bitcoin allows users to send digital cash to different users without having to use a financial intermediary for contracts that are completed correctly. But, a miner is someone who is going to be adding blocks to the block chain and collects a reward for the work done when intermediaries are found in bitcoin.

However, one miner can be released while another moves so that the work that needs to be done gets done.

Private block chains have middlemen, though. These people are the ones who are going to be running nodes or the technology needed to clip tickets so that they can monetize the block chain solutions.

**Four: users are able to run block chains off their phones**

Using your phone to store block chain data is something that needs to be approached with caution. In using a phone, your phone is going to continuously chat with the rest of the block chain network while downloading as well as uploading other user's data constantly in order to stay in consensus.

## Five: Block chain will contain a constant record of all events

Old transactions sometimes need to be tracked so that new transactions can be validated this also happens when the transaction is broadcasted across the bitcoin network in order to be added into a block on the chain. Every event that happens within bitcoin is going to build up an image in order to show an accurate picture of the ledger.

But, this is not going to mean that you will be able to fix random problems with block chains or that these problems are going to give an accurate image of every event instantly. Events are going to need to be inputted by an individual or by a program so that it can be broadcasted before being accepted and recorded onto a block.

The data that is on blocks is not going to be uploaded and accurate automatically. Events are going to need to be recorded properly in the first place before they are going to be broadcasted accurately. If the record is immutable, then the accuracy is going to be essential.

## Six: If it's on block chain, it's true

The word true on block chain simply means that the network agreed the transaction took place and that the nodes have agreed on the transaction. But, the meaning of the word true on block chain does not mean the same thing as the other meanings of the word true. For example, if a heart monitor records inaccurate data onto a block then that data is will be the truth because it was not what actually took place. In many cases, true simply means that the information that was recorded was validated by the majority of nodes. However, this validity does not necessarily mean that it is true.

## Seven: data that is stored in a block chain

Data is prevalent with the block chains that are used for document storage or for KYC. The comments of "This is stored on block chain" actually can cause some confusion when it comes to a document being published on a block chain. Hash documents are not encrypted so when it is stored within a block; you are not going to be able to retrieve the original document through the process of decrypting the hash.

If a hash is stored on block chain, then someone has kept the original data so that they can help prove the data actually exists as well as the timestamp of when the data was placed onto the block chain.

In storing whole documents on block chain, large chunks of data are going to be passed around at a speed that will create a whole new set of problems.

## Eight: Participants to a block chain

The word participant is often confused when looking at who actually participates in block chain. However, looking at those who participate in block chain, there are three main participants.

- There are those who are the end users. These participants are those who usually access the block chain by linking to a node that is full. In bitcoin, these participants are called users.
- Participants who write blocks are considered to be the miners who crunch numbers and actually do the work that a smart contract is made out for.
- Then there are the users who maintain the entirety of block chain and help to validate new entries. Generally, these are called full nodes.

## Nine: what should block chain be used for?

## *Block Chain*

Block chain is particularly great with multiple parties that are needing information read for whatever reason. However, there is not one specific party that is in control of the data.

*Block Chain*

# Chapter Twelve: Myths about Block Chain and Bitcoin

Since block chain is still a bit of a mystery, there are myths that surround block chain and bitcoin. However, these myths can cause someone to not want to invest with block chain because they will not be sure about block chain. In this section, we are going to bust through some of those myths to help make block chain a little easier to understand and hopefully entice you into investing with it.

**One:** Block chain is a decenertralized ledger that is able to be split apart from bitcoin.

Many people will argue that bitcoin has failed as a currency where block chain happened to work. Along those lines, they are then able to conclude that the block chain can be isolated and rebuilt on a decentralized transaction system. These thoughts are nothing short of absurd.

When looking at reality, you will realize that block chain is already a strongly decentralized system, and this happens because of the bitcoin encryption algorithms as well as the network protocols that will ultimately determine how a miner is to verify as well as validate their transactions.

Much like Bitcoin, systems like Ethereum can develop their own block chain. However, bitcoin is the only true decentralized system that will not need supervision.

**Two:** Bitcoin is used by tens of thousands of legal merchants.

There are not many merchants that actually accept bitcoin. About eighty percent of bitcoin currency is used for speculative hoarding. The best that a merchant can do is to allow you to use your bitcoins in a partnering facility that will then turn them into dollars. The exchange costs, as well as any other risks, are going to be on you.

The merchants that do accept bitcoin are going to check out how it works and if it is beneficial to them. They will also accept bitcoins in order to look cool or to get more media exposure so that they are able to gain more customers.

**Three:** Bitcoin transactions can be processed in real time

If you remember earlier it was stated that blocks are usually done in ten-minute increments, then you know how long the bitcoin transactions are processed. Less than two transactions are made per second on the bitcoin network when compared to the visa transactions that are made.

**Four:** Bitcoin transactions are "nearly free."

The processing fee from bitcoin transactions is not charged to the users, but it is not charged to the merchants either.

Miners are able to process transactions and they are currently making well over ninety-nine percent of their revenue from mining the new bitcoins. This is going to happen until the twenty-one million bitcoins are mined which is planned to happen around 2140. However, there are no clear plans as to what the transaction costs will be after this has been reached.

Transaction processing is rewarded through the network in small amounts, but this represents about less than one percent of the miner's actual revenue. The total of miner rewards will ultimately warrant the high amount of investment costs as well as operating costs that mining brings up. Therefore, the cost of a transaction is going to take all of the mining cost into account. For example, if it is 7.52 per transaction, there will be an average of 764 dollars.

As soon as exchange commissions have been added in, the cost will no longer be negligible.

**Five:** Bitcoin is more secure

Bitcoin has a high resilience against attacks. But, similar to any other transaction system, there are going to be security breaches that are going to be cause by simple human failure as well as fraud.

In 2015:

- Bitcoin lost about two million dollars due to a phishing attack
- Bitstamp had to temporarily suspend trading due to the operation of one of their wallets being compromised.
- The Canadian bitcoin exchange had to shut down due to a compromise in their database.
- Three hundred and eighty-seven million dollars in client funds vanished from the Hong Kong bitcoin exchange.

**Six:** Bitcoin's ecosystem is decentralized

Bitcoin has increased in a few mining pools. The four leading ones actually include having three that are from the China bitcoin exchange which is about seventy-five percent controled by hashing.

The large mining farms are artificially limited themselvs, so there is no illusion of any democracy. However, smaller miners and mining pools are being driven out of business by the larger mining farms.

The true reason for this dominance is that by generating bitcoins through the use of mining has become harder since the number of bitcoins has increased. The larger farms are able to afford the high investment and operating prices that mining will require.

Bitcoin is controlled by a few opaque players that have about fifty-one percent of the majority that will then allow them to modify transaction rules.

**Seven:** Bitcoin is idealistic as well as non-profit.

Millions of dollars' worth of investments are actually riding on bitcoin. There are about five billion dollars cumulated within bitcoin currency. Not only that, but here are billions of dollars that have been invested when it comes to mining, wallet operations, and exchanges.

Some examples would be:

- Bitcoin startup not being in stealth mode, 21 Inc has raised about one hundred and sixteen million dollars from the VCs in Sillicon Valley
- Coinbase has raised one hundred million dollars.
- Goldman Sachs has also invested about fifty million dollars in bitcoin startup and they have called it Circle.

# Chapter Thirteen: Block chain terms

There are terms when using block chain that you will need to need to know in order to use bitcoin and block chain to your benefit.

**Address:** this is used to receive as well as send transactions on the network. The address is going to contain a string of alphanumeric characters as well as contain a scannable QR code. The bitcoin address is much like a set of keys. There is going to be a public key that a user is going to hold in order to sign their transactions digitally.

**Bitcoin ATM:** a bitcoin ATM is much like an ATM. It is a physical machine that is going to allow a customer to purchase bitcoin with their own cash. Many manufacturers are enabling users to sell bitcoins for cash as well. Sometimes these are called BTMs or even Bitcoin AVMS.

**Bitcoin Price Index (BPI):** BPI is a representation of the average price of bitcoin across the leading global exchange. But, it must meet the criteria that has been specified by the BPI.

**BitPay:** this is a payment processor that is used for bitcoins. It works with merchants by allowing them to take bitcoin as payment.

**Block chain:** there is a full list of blocks that have been mined since bitcoin cryptocurrency has started. The block chain was designed so that every block holds a drawing on the blocks that came before it. This was designed in order to make I tamperproof.

**Block reward:** this is a reward that is given to the miner for successfully completing a transaction block. There is going to be a mixture of coins as well as transaction fees that are going to follow the policy of the cryptocurrency that is being used. It will also be dependent on if all the coins have been successfully mined. For every block that is mined, there is a reward of twenty-five bitcoins. The block is going to give half of the reward until a certain number of blocks have been mined.

**Client:** the client is a software program that is going to run on a computer or mobile device. This is going to help connect the computer or mobile device to the bitcoin network and forward the transactions.

**Cryptocurrency:** a form of currency that is solely based on mathematics. Cryptocurrency is not printed currency, and it is produced by the solving of the mathematical problems that come from cryptography.

**Cryptography:** using mathematics, cryptography is able to create codes as well as ciphers that are going to help conceal any information so that it can be verified and secured.

**Exchange:** the central resource used for exchanging different forms of money and a variety of other assets. The bitcoin exchanges are going to be used to exchange cryptocurrency. Normally it is used to trade fiat currency.

**Fiat currency:** this currency is made out of thin air and only contains value because people say it does. Fiat currency is under close scrutiny by regulators because of the known application it has in money laundering as well as various terrorist attacks. This is not to be confused with bitcoin.

## Block Chain

**Hash:** Hash is a mathematical process that is going to take the variable amount of data that it is given in order to produce a shorter output. The hashing function actually has two very important characteristics. First, it is mathematically difficult to be able to work out what the original input was by simply looking at the output. Next, in changing a small part of the input is going to give you an entirely different output.

**Hash rate:** the number of hashes that a bitcoin miner can produce in a specified amount of time.

**Input:** the bitcoin payment comes from this part of the bitcoin transaction. Usually, the bitcoin address is going to be the input unless a transaction generates one. In simpler terms, unless the bitcoin is mined, the input is going to be the bitcoin address.

**KYC:** Know your client/customer.

**Mining:** this is the act that is known for generating new bitcoins. This process is done by solving the cryptographic problems through the use of computer hardware.

**Node:** when a computer is connected to the bitcoin network, then the client will be transmitting multiple transactions to the clients.

**Output:** the final destination where the address is going to be in a bitcoin transaction. A single transaction can have multiple outputs.

**Pre-mining:** a coin can be mined before the coin has even been announced. Pre-mining happens to be a common technique that scamcoins use. But, pre-mined coins are not always going to be scamcoins.

**Private key:** an alphanumeric string that is kept private by the user that it is assigned to. It is meant as a means of

## Block Chain

sending out a digital signature when hashed with a public key. In many cases, this string is going to be a private key that is designed in order to work with a public key. The public key is going to be the bitcoin address.

**Proof of work:** a system ties mining capability to computational power. The blocks are going to need to be hashed with an easy computational process. But, there is an additional variable that is going to be added to the process that is going to make it more difficult. Once a block has successfully been hashed, then the hashing is to be the proof of work that is needed for a block be validated.

**Public key:** this is a key that is publicly known with a hashed block. It is also known as the bitcoin address.

**Scamcoin:** an altcoin that is produced for the sole purpose of making money for the originator of the coin. These are often used in pump and dump techniques as well as pre-mining.

**Transaction fee:** there is a fee that is imposed on various transactions that happen on the bitcoin network. This fee is going to be award to the miner that successfully minds the block that holds the relevant transaction.

**Wallet:** this is a method used for storing coins for later use.

# Chapter Fourteen: Block chain and Etherum

Block chain is used in Etherum as well since Etherum uses cryptocurrency that is similar to bitcoins.

Ethereum is a block chain platform that is public and has a programmable transaction functionality. In other words, Ethereum decentralizes and provides a peer to peer contract by using cryptocurrency that is known as Ether.

Ethereum was first proposed late in the year during 2013 by a man named Vitalik Buterin. However, this next generation cryptocurrency and decentralized application platform were funded and developed in August of 2014.

Buterin is a Russian-Canadian programmer that is also involved in working with Bitcoin. Instead of working on the Bitcoin protocol, Ethereum actually creates its own block chain in order to provide a greater developmental flexibility. It does this by using a Turing-complete programming language.

While it was being developed in 2014, the developers described it as a program that would extend the block chain beyond the peer to peer system that Bitcoin used. Just as with any project, questions were raised about the scalability as well as the security of Ethereum. However, still in 2014, the World Technology Award was given to Buterin for helping invent Ethereum.

July 30 of 2015, Ethereum's block chain went live and was launched. Originally, the program was developed by the Swiss company Ethereum Switzerland GmbH as well as a Swiss non-profit foundation known as the Ethereum Foundation.

## Block Chain

Once May of 2016 came around, the value token, ether, was worth north of one billion dollars. Vox noted the new currency was a challenge to bitcoin in the simple fact that it offered a different range of uses that bitcoin was unable to offer.

Many people don't know that there is more than just bitcoin and ethereum for you to choose from when it comes to cryptocurrency. In a later chapter, you will find a few resources that you can use to find the cryptocurrency that is best for you.

Just like with Bitcoin, you are able to invest using the Ethereum platform. It was mentioned above that both Bitcoin and Ethereum use block chains in order to save their transactions. However, with Ethereum being new, there will be some differences that the user will not be used to like they are with the Bitcoin platform.

Many people wonder if Ethereum is going to surpass Bitcoin because of the different platform that it offers the users and the new developments that the coders and other employees are coming up with as far as advancing Ethereum goes. But, just like with Bitcoin, you can invest using this platform and have access to the different cryptocurrencies as well as the ability to exchange them.

So, what makes Ethereum different? As previously stated, Ethereum is a decentralized platform that allows applications to run autonomously and offers the risk of downtime, fraud, third party interferences, and censorship to be non-existent. Ultimately, this means that when you're investing, you're not going to find the restraints with Ethereum that you might find with another platform such as Bitcoin.

Before you can invest with Ethereum, you have to understand how it works. Ethereum works off of contracts

*Block Chain*

that unlock values should different conditions be met. For example, if user A is to go to a specific website a certain number of times, then they are to do this in order to meet the conditions of the contract that was set up by user B. Once they have met the conditions, they will be rewarded with one Ether (Ethereum cryptocurrency) in exchange for their work. This payment is sent out immediately and does not require a second transaction. Also, ownerships of programs can be transferred from user to user with the block chain system. In other words, the contracts can be traded between users as well.

# Conclusion

Thank you again for downloading this book!

I hope this book was able to give you a bit more information on how block chain works as well as the basics of how bitcoin mining works.

The next step is to either join in on the bitcoin society or if block chain would be a program that would help you with something that you are currently working on or with. (Keep in mind that block chain is a system that relies on itself and its users.)

Finally, if you enjoyed this book, please take the time to share your thoughts and post a review on Amazon. It'd be greatly appreciated!

Thank you and good luck!

# References:

DECORATIVE BUILDING BLOCKS - Mcerlean, James Murray. (n.d.). Retrieved from http://www.sumobrain.com/patents/wipo/Decorative-building-blocks/WO2004072401.ht

Block chain Disrupting the Financial Engaging title in ... (n.d.). Retrieved from https://www2.deloitte.com/content/dam/Deloitte/ie/Documents/FinancialServices/IE

Business Object Question | Coffeehouse | Forums | Channel 9. (n.d.). Retrieved from https://channel9.msdn.com/Forums/Coffeehouse/41828-Business-Object-Question

Cryptocurrency - Wikipedia, the free encyclopedia. (n.d.). Retrieved from https://en.wikipedia.org/wiki/Cryptocurrency

Smart Contracts: How to Use Block chain... - amazon.co.uk. (n.d.). Retrieved from https://www.amazon.co.uk/Smart-Contracts-Block chain-Cryptocurrency-Exchange/dp/1

8452 SPI - Tristate output line - Discussion Forums ... (n.d.). Retrieved from http://forums.ni.com/t5/Instrument-Control-GPIB-Serial/8452-SPI-Tristate-output-

Bitcoin Glossary & Frequently Asked Questions. (n.d.). Retrieved from https://99bitcoins.com/bitcoin-glossary-faq/

www.ingramcontent.com/pod-product-compliance
Lightning Source LLC
Chambersburg PA
CBHW070407190526
45169CB00003B/1153